WHEN
I AM AN
OLD
COOT

WHEN I AM AN OLD COOT

ROY ENGLISH

GIBBS·SMITH
P
PUBLISHER

Salt Lake City

04 03 02 01   9   8   7   6

Text copyright © 1995 by Roy English
Flip cartoon illustrations by Steve Egan,
© 1995 by Gibbs Smith, Publisher.

Published by
Gibbs Smith, Publisher
P.O. Box 667
Layton, Utah 84041

Interior design by Mary Ellen Thompson
Cover design by Steve Jerman
Animation by Steve Egan, © 1995 by Gibbs Smith,
Publisher

Printed and bound in the U.S.A.

Library of Congress Cataloging-in-Publication Data

English, Roy, 1943-
When I am an old coot— / Roy English.

p. cm.
ISBN 0-87905-695-9
1. Aging—Humor. I. Title.
PN6231.A43E54   1995
818' .5402-dc20   95-13153
                                   CIP

TO OLD COOTS
AND FREE SPIRITS—
LONG MAY THEY DANCE.

WHEN I AM AN OLD COOT . . .

I will wear funny hats
and loud ties,
flowered underwear
and bright
yellow suspenders.
I will break all the silly,
proper rules and
be a kid again.

I will teach young children the joys of blowing Jell-O on their little friends.

7

WHEN I AM AN OLD COOT . . .

I will pierce my ear
and wear a pico perch in
case someone wants
to go fishing.

I will carry my own trail mix of salted peanuts, Junior Mints, candy corn, and Rolaids.

WHEN I AM AN OLD COOT . . .

I will perform my civic
duty by making sure all
the residents at The Home
are registered to vote.
I will, of course, collect a
small poll tax
for my trouble.

I will ride a
Harley Davidson hog
in funeral processions
of old golfing buddies and
deserving friends.

WHEN I AM AN OLD COOT . . .

I will make a will
and donate my bones
to the Museum
of Archaeology
to be exhibited as a
"Fartasaurus Rex."

I will carry my

sleeping bag

to doctor appointments

and nap on the floor

in the waiting room.

WHEN I AM AN OLD COOT . . .

I will open a restaurant
featuring low-fat, no-salt,
low-cholesterol foods.
I will hire healthy young
waitresses and call
the place "Cooters."

I will go to the Dairy Queen
and dip my dentures in
the hot fudge when the
waitress isn't looking.

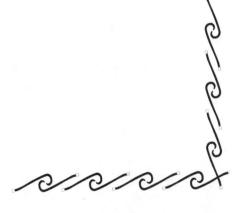

WHEN I AM AN OLD COOT . . .

I will trick my
forgetful friends
at The Home by giving
myself a birthday party
several times a year and
asking them to bring gifts.

I will go to a

country-western nightclub

and scatter the

line dancers with my

personal version of the

"Poot Scootin' Boogie."

WHEN I AM AN OLD COOT . . .

I will rent a limo for the day
and show up at busy offices
all over town, introduce
myself as the new owner,
and give everyone
the day off.

I will call *A Current Affair*

and ask them how

I can order one.

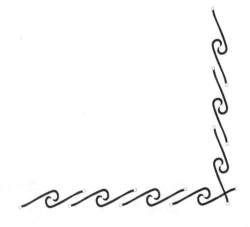

WHEN I AM AN OLD COOT . . .

I will stroll proudly through
the maternity ward
carrying a stuffed bear
and passing out cigars.

I will engage telephone solicitors in endless conversation and discussion of my traumatic personal problems until they hang up on me.

WHEN I AM AN OLD COOT . . .

I will go to baseball-card
conventions. I will put a big
chew of tobacco in my cheek
and walk around spitting
on the floor and
grabbing myself and
claim to have pitched in the
1939 World Series.

I will enroll in
junior college and
argue with the history teacher
when she gets it wrong.

WHEN I AM AN OLD COOT . . .

I will write to the Preparation-H company and thank them from the heart of my bottom.

I will rent a gorilla suit
and wear it to the zoo
and jump out at people
from behind trees and
grab their popcorn.

WHEN I AM AN OLD COOT . . .

I will buy a fishing cabin
on a river and finance it
with a 30-year mortgage so
my children will
remember me
when I'm gone.

I will drive to West Texas for the fall foliage tour. Since everyone else will be in New England or the Rockies, there won't be much traffic. Of course, there won't be much foliage either.

WHEN I AM AN OLD COOT . . .

I will teach my dog to fetch my neighbor's morning newspaper, but I will always return it after I have read the sports and comics.

I will petition the city council

to return the zoo animals

to the wilds and convert

the zoo into a jail

so we can keep

the right critters

locked up.

WHEN I AM AN OLD COOT . . .

I will watch all the
old western movies again.
This time I will
root for the Indians.

I will hitchhike from

time to time

to see what kind of person

will give an old codger

a ride.

WHEN I AM AN OLD COOT . . .

I will assess a

two-stroke penalty to

any of my old

golfing partners who require

medical attention

or have to relieve themselves

in the middle of a round.

I will tell the grandkids
my TV is broken
so they will have to
listen to my stories.

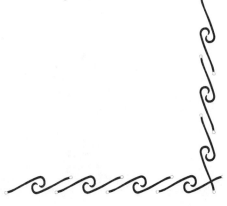

WHEN I AM AN OLD COOT . . .

I will invite every woman
I know to the top
of the Empire State Building
and ask them if
we ever had
"an affair I can't remember."

I will keep a can of earthworms and a bucket of minnows in my refrigerator.

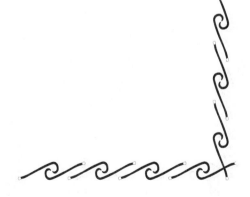

WHEN I AM AN OLD COOT . . .

I will track down
Willie Nelson and tell him
I was wrong and he was right
about some things.

I will let my

nose hair grow

so I can

tickle my sweetheart.

WHEN I AM AN OLD COOT . . .

I will drink cold milk from
the jug and iced tea from
the pitcher. I will eat
blackberries from the vine,
green onions from the ground,
and peaches from the tree,
but I will not eat liver.

I will give all my stuff away.
I will not own
anything that eats
(except for one old dog
and a cat), nor will I
own anything that is subject
to government inspection
or property taxes.

WHEN I AM AN OLD COOT . . .

I will prepare a special dinner
for myself every Friday night.
I will serve spaghetti with
tomato sauce and garlic bread.
I will sip red wine and
sing along with Pavarotti
and toast dear friends,
alive and dead.

I will sit in the cafeteria
and argue loudly with myself
about whether my meal
"tasted great"
or was "less filling."

WHEN I AM AN OLD COOT . . .

I will take my pooper scooper
and transfer the products
of my neighbor's Great Dane
from my front yard
to the hood of his Buick.

I will get up during the night,
slip on my Nike's,
and "just do it."

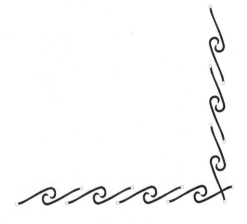

WHEN I AM AN OLD COOT . . .

I will insist on sitting
on Santa's knee
at the department store,
then throw a squalling fit
about the pony I didn't get
when I was six.

I will spray air freshener around old women who smell like flower gardens.

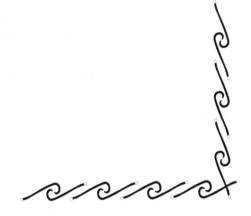

WHEN I AM AN OLD COOT . . .

I will hide bananas
and chocolate brownies
in my sock drawer
and keep a jar
of peanut butter
under my bed.

I will smile sweetly

at strangers and

offer to share

the peppermint stick

that I have been licking.

WHEN I AM AN OLD COOT . . .

I will use my tweezers
to poke bird droppings
into a cigarette
and wait for
my worthless nephew
to bum a smoke again.

I will carry a bottle of
Listerine to my dentist's office
and tell him I will gargle
if he will.

49

WHEN I AM AN OLD COOT . . .

I will handcuff my wheelchair
to the ice-cream truck
until the company agrees
to make tutti-fruiti again.

I will put a Coke bottle
in my pants pocket
and tell my nurse
"it's the real thing."

WHEN I AM AN OLD COOT . . .

I will appear on
The Wheel of Fortune,
and, when I solve a puzzle,
I will break down
and sobbingly confess
that the game is rigged
and that Vanna gave me
the answer for half the loot.

I will disguise my voice

as Ed McMahan

and leave messages

on answering machines from

Publishers Clearing House

that I have great news.

WHEN I AM AN OLD COOT . . .

I will carry my putter
wherever I go
and use it as a cane,
back scratcher, and
all-purpose whacker.
Sometimes I will
flail it around like
Chi Chi Rodriguez.

I will have power lunches
with my cat
at Long John Silver.

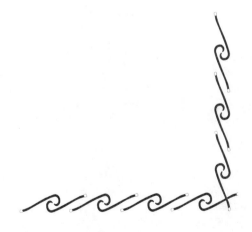

WHEN I AM AN OLD COOT . . .

I will growl at
nervous little dogs
in public places
and make them
bark frantically.

I will wrestle old,
worn-out dogs
and pretend to
let them pin me.

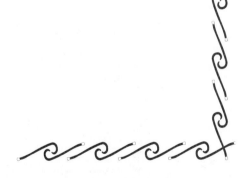

WHEN I AM AN OLD COOT . . .

I will disinherit my kids
and leave all my
worldly possessions
to the lady who
changes my covers
and gives me a bath.

I will dawdle by the
cleaning lady,
pretend to stumble,
and grab her buttocks firmly.

WHEN I AM AN OLD COOT . . .

I will camp beneath the

stars in City Park

and eat beans from a can

and chew tobacco.

I will sing

"Home on the Range"

and pee on the smoldering

campfire to make it sizzle.

⊥

I will procure a
white jacket and stethoscope
and roam the halls
of the hospital
acting important.

WHEN I AM AN OLD COOT . . .

I will attend public meetings
and raise hell with officials
about whatever is
on the agenda.

I will break wind
in public places
and frown disgustedly
at the fellow beside me.

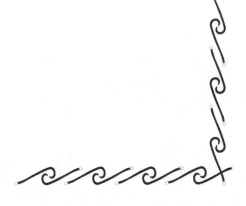

WHEN I AM AN OLD COOT . . .

I will attend fancy art auctions,

sip champagne and munch

little watercress sandwiches,

and bid on Van Goghs

and Picassos.

Then, if I am the high bidder,

I will blame it on my

dandruff and itchy scalp.

I will smoke

Rum Crook cigars

in airline lavatories

and dare the flight attendant

to throw me off the plane.

Every Columbus Day
I will walk
around the courthouse
with a sign that says
"Indians Discovered America."

I will fake an asthma attack
and break into a fit of
loud coughing when
the preacher talks too long
and the Cowboys have
a noon kickoff on TV.

WHEN I AM AN OLD COOT . . .

I will send flowers and candy
to myself and display them
before my friends at The Home.
They will come with
little cards signed by
such dear friends as
Hillary, Oprah,
and Princess Di.

I will write letters to the editor

extolling the joys

and social benefits

of prostitution

and sign the mayor's name.

WHEN I AM AN OLD COOT . . .

I will teach the children
to belch "Clementine"
when their mommies
are not around.

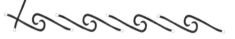

I will stroll around Graceland

in a white jumpsuit

and introduce myself

as Elvis's uncle.

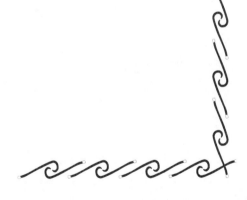

WHEN I AM AN OLD COOT . . .

I will pretend to be
an inspector from
the Wildlife Commission
and go fishing
at the hatchery.

I will go to confession
and make up wild stories
about the local parishioners
and never admit to
being a Presbyterian.

WHEN I AM AN OLD COOT . . .

I will wear hip waders
and carry a fly rod
and fish the fountains
in front of Caesar's Palace.

I will go bowling

and play poker with the boys

and eat prunes

and be a regular guy.

WHEN I AM AN OLD COOT . . .

I will hook a pair of Huskies
to my wheelchair
and pretend to be
Charlton Heston.

I will safety-pin my socks
together when I wash them
so the blue ones
and black ones
don't try to mate.

WHEN I AM AN OLD COOT . . .

I will drop my dentures
into the punch bowl
at parties when
I think the others
have had enough.

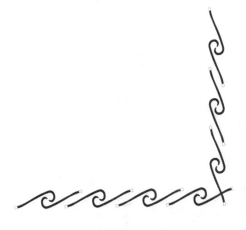

I will butter my pills
so they don't get hung
in my esophagus.

WHEN I AM AN OLD COOT . . .

I will lobby the legislature

for a sin tax

on ice cream and donuts.

They have done me more harm

than cigarettes and whiskey.

I will teach the children
not to gamble
by cheating them
in little card games and
taking their lunch money.

I will rescue bird-dogs
from those
tiny little cages.

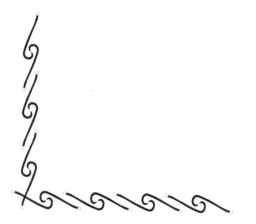

I will file a complaint
against my proctologist
for trespassing
and unlawful entry.

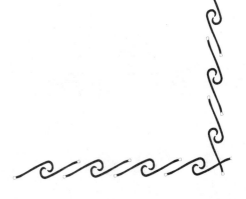

WHEN I AM AN OLD COOT . . .

I will rig up a little bungee jump for my neighbor's yelping Chihuahua.

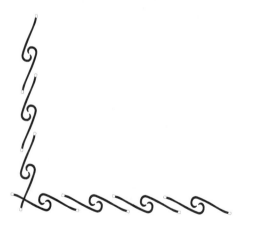

I will pierce my nostril
and entertain the children
by blowing my nose
like a whale.

WHEN I AM AN OLD COOT . . .

I will trick my friends
at The Home by standing at
the door and collecting a small
admission for various
little programs the
church presents.

I will take steam baths
and stroll naked around
the locker room and
hang out with my buddies.

WHEN I AM AN OLD COOT . . .

I will carry a bucket of paint
in the back
of my pickup truck and
create handicap parking spaces
wherever I think
they should be.

I will put expensive price tags

on cheap gifts

and pretend that

I forgot to take them off.

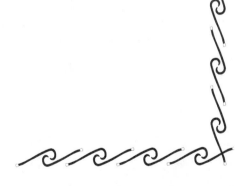

WHEN I AM AN OLD COOT . . .

I will show up at
wedding receptions
and stuff myself
with fancy hors d'oeuvres
and whisper nasty little
comments about the
groom's family secrets.

I will ask people
for directions
and then argue
with them.

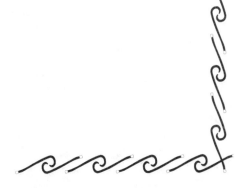

WHEN I AM AN OLD COOT . . .

I will tell all my family
members that,
for my next birthday,
I would like to receive cash
instead of socks and ties.

I will promptly return
the handkerchiefs that
I borrow to clean my ears
and blow my nose.

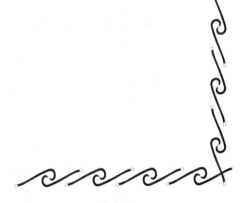

WHEN I AM AN OLD COOT . . .

I will join the
volunteer fire department
and put emergency lights and
a siren on my pickup truck.
I will use them often
to make sure
they are working properly.

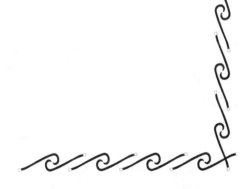

I will carry a little

whisk broom

and brush the dandruff from

people's shoulders.

WHEN I AM AN OLD COOT . . .

I will save my used
dental floss
to tie bows and name tags
on little gifts.

I will invite

David Letterman's mama

to cover the

"Old Coot Winter Olympics"

in Miami.

WHEN I AM AN OLD COOT . . .

I will carry

dried dog and cat food

in the back of my truck

for old strays

that I come across.

I will occasionally
ride a broomstick to breakfast
and insist that
the cafeteria lady bring
an extra bowl of oats
for my horse.

WHEN I AM AN OLD COOT . . .

I will write the
Quarter Horse Association and
nominate the electric company
as "Stud of the Year"
for the way it
services its customers.

I will go to the Gourmet
Room at the Ritz-Carlton and
order a pitcher of buttermilk
and half a cantaloupe
full of chili.

WHEN I AM AN OLD COOT . . .

I will sit in the
Little League stands
and yell instructions
to every coach and player
on the field.

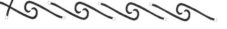

I will get down on my knees

from time to time

and try to sneak up on

old dogs, grandkids,

brook trout, and

The Good Lord.

WHEN I AM AN OLD COOT . . .

I will stand up at
the Sportsmen's Banquet
and announce
that the best way to have
"ducks unlimited"
is to stop
shooting their butts off.

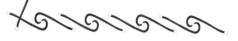

I will get out my old
school pictures and toast
the memory of Mrs. May,
my third grade teacher,
and tell her I still love her.

WHEN I AM AN OLD COOT . . .

I will dance with my wife
in the kitchen
and nibble her ear
and make her giggle.
I will write little poems for her
and thank her for being
a saint and a soldier.

I will introduce my
grandchildren to the
rhythm and blues
of Lightning Hopkins
and Jimmy Reed.

WHEN I AM AN OLD COOT . . .

I will carry a styrofoam cooler
with artichokes, anchovies,
jalapeños, and Grey Poupon
to add zest to fast foods.
I will also carry
a bottle of Maalox.

I will learn to play the harmonica like a freight train and make up hobo stories about riding the rails with Box Car Willie.

WHEN I AM AN OLD COOT . . .

I will reserve a window seat on the flight into Dulles International and moon Congress from 40,000 feet.

I will borrow a bailiff's uniform

and frisk prospective jurors

as they arrive

at the courthouse.

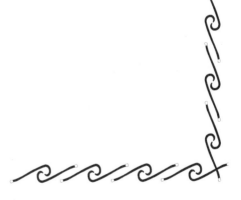

WHEN I AM AN OLD COOT . . .

I will call that TV preacher
who hustles everybody
and tell him my prayer request
is that he get an honest job.

I will carry toothpicks for friends who occasionally have green vegetables hanging from their teeth.

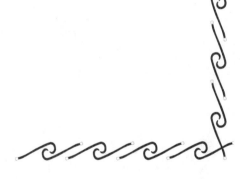

WHEN I AM AN OLD COOT . . .

And I hit a bad golf shot,
I will claim that someone
broke wind
during my backswing
and distracted me.
I will demand a mulligan.

I will demonstrate my
dexterity and steady hand
by eating peas
with a table knife.

115

WHEN I AM AN OLD COOT . . .

I will police the
express check-out line
at the supermarket
and deny entry to anyone
with more than ten items.

I will hop on my snowmobile and "kick ice" across the mountain.

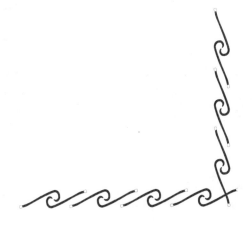

WHEN I AM AN OLD COOT . . .

I will eat blue-corn tortillas
and refried beans
and sit by the campfire
and sing, "You are the wind
beneath my jeans."

I will stroll through
the cemetery singing,
"I've got friends in low places."

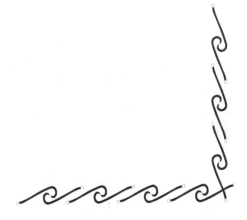

WHEN I AM AN OLD COOT . . .

I will go to the Super Bowl

and slip onto the field

at halftime and

play my trombone

with the marching band

on national TV.

I will spend the second half

of the game in jail.

I will knit Michael Jackson

another glove

so he won't keep shivering

and grabbing himself

to get warm.

WHEN I AM AN OLD COOT . . .

I will go back to
Luckenbach, Texas, and play
dominoes with Willie and
Waylon and the boys, and
keep an eye out
for Emmylou.

I will carry a black robe
and Bible and administer
the wedding vows
to any couple who
appears to need marrying.

WHEN I AM AN OLD COOT . . .

I will stand on a phone book at girlie shows in case I want to reach out and touch someone.

I will test the patience
of my golfing partners
by taking little naps
while frozen over
important putts.

WHEN I AM AN OLD COOT . . .

I will go to Billy Bob's
Honky-Tonk and have that
shoe-shine cowgirl
shine the dance
back into my boots.

I will save a lot of money
on barbers.

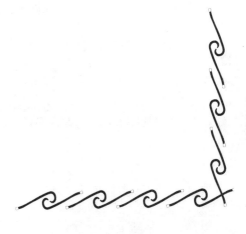

WHEN I AM AN OLD COOT . . .

I will take a trailer of

young farm animals

to the inner-city park and

give every kid the chance

to ride a pony,

pet a rabbit,

and scratch a pig's ear.

I will open the
Polyester Wax Museum
at The Home
and get my domino pals
to hold a pose when
paying customers arrive.

WHEN I AM AN OLD COOT . . .

I will refuse to grow old gracefully and will leave this world like I came in— kicking, squalling, and raising a stink.

I will ask my young nurse
if she would like to
jump-start my pacemaker.

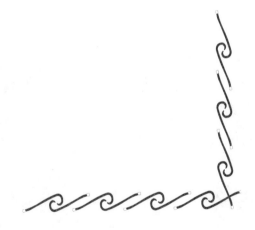

WHEN I AM AN OLD COOT . . .

I will recruit my friends in
rockers and wheelchairs
and form a rock 'n' roll band.
We will call our group
"The Rolling Kidney Stones."
Our fans will be called
"Cooties."

I will give the little ladies
at The Home a thrill
by asking if they would like to
go steady and swap dentures.

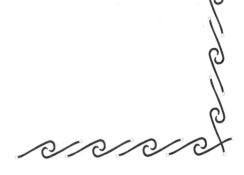

WHEN I AM AN OLD COOT . . .

I will distribute hammers to
residents at The Home
so they can open those little
tamper-proof pill bottles their
medicine comes in.

I will double up on the Old Spice when I haven't showered for a few days.

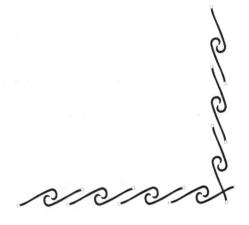

WHEN I AM AN OLD COOT . . .

I will burn my
Christmas lights all year, put
a jack-o'-lantern in my window,
and erect an eight-foot
Easter bunny in the front yard
beside my cardboard
Clint Eastwood.

I will attend wedding
receptions and lick the knife
for good luck
before the bride and groom
cut the cake.

WHEN I AM AN OLD COOT . . .

I will wear two neckties on
special occasions.

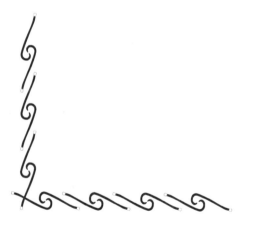

I will slip an Alka Seltzer

inside my cheek

and tell the nurse

I think I have rabies.

WHEN I AM AN OLD COOT . . .

I will stop searching

and proclaim

that I have found myself,

and I am pretty silly.

I will go to antique auctions
and try to sell my body.

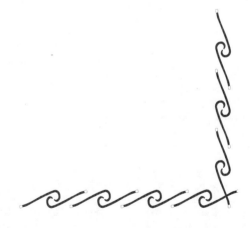

WHEN I AM AN OLD COOT . . .

I will take my bedroll
to the Farmers Market and
curl up in the fragrant shade
of a load of ripe cantaloupes
and let my nose
take me back to Grandpa.

I will practice "Cootspa"
to get my way:
from outrageous charm to
cantankerous intimidation.

WHEN I AM AN OLD COOT . . .

I will take little trips
inside my head and visit
with departed friends.
I will dance with angels
whenever I hear the music.

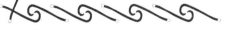